Let's fly into this book

First Published 2025 by Jenny Dyer
For further information
contact through facebook page

Walking with Wildlife

or website

www.walkingwithwildlife.com.au

Text: © Jennifer Dyer 2025
Photography: © Jennifer Dyer 2024

All rights reserved. No part of this publication may be reproduced, stored in a retrieval system, or transmitted in any form or by any means electronic or mechanical, or by photocopying or otherwise without prior written permission of the author or copyright holder.

ISBN 978-1-7637939-9-6

Cover and Artwork: Jenny Dyer

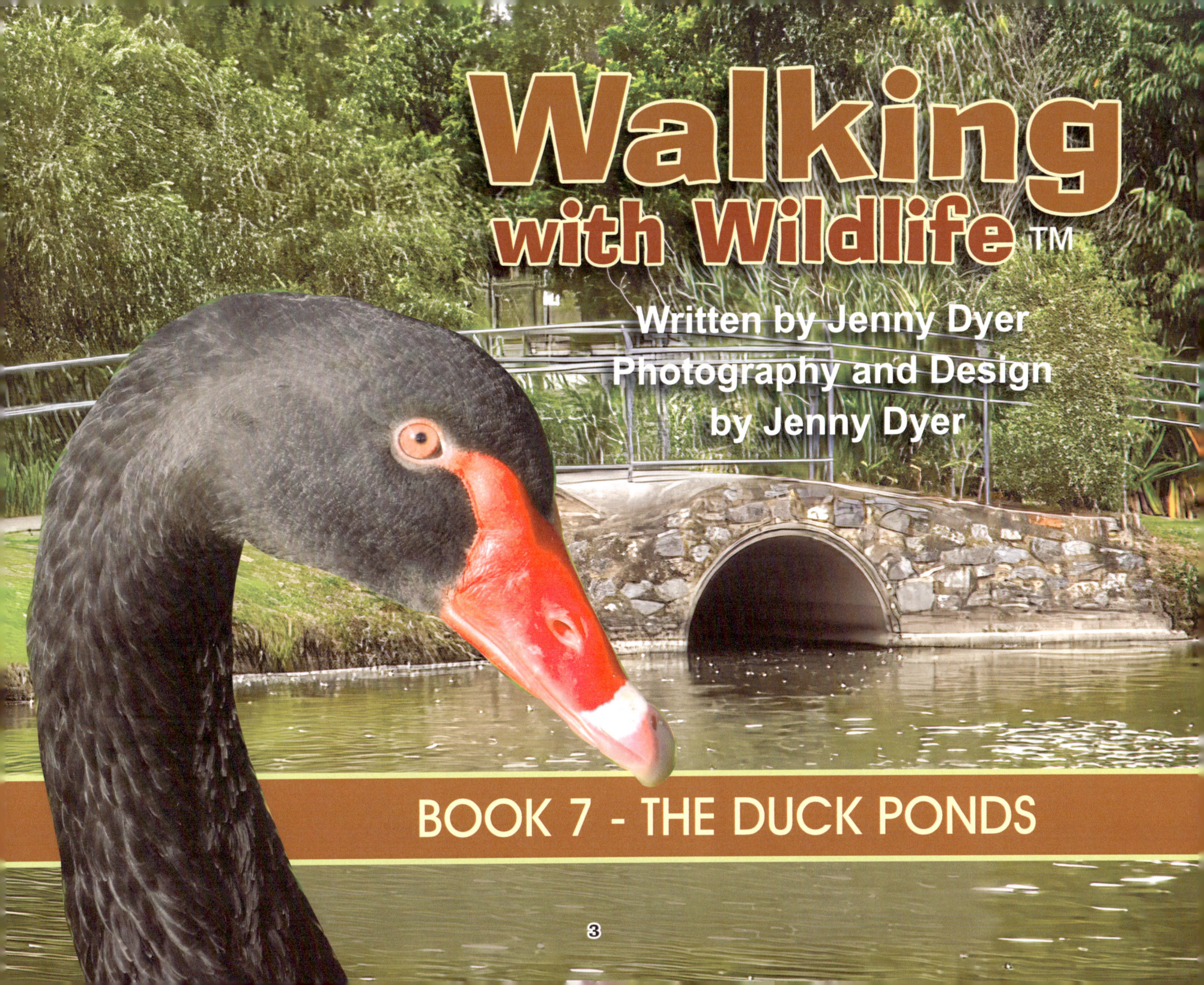

For today's adventure we change our location from my bush track to the duck ponds where I can see the water birds. The swans and their babies, called cygnets, are a delight to watch.

We were very lucky to be there as the swans went for a swim with their cute, fluffy cygnets.

Until they are able to swim safely alone, tiny cygnets are carried on their mother's back to keep them safe and warm. These ones are old enough to swim by themselves.

Both the male and female swans care for their cygnets and are very protective of them if any other birds venture close.

Mum and Dad swan are never far away.

The cygnets leave their parents sometime between four and twelve months old. At this stage they are grey and brown.

This swan struggled and flapped its wings to go ashore. These large birds can be very clumsy on land.

When swans make a heart shape they aren't "in love". They are actually two males trying to prove who is the boss.

Sometimes you may witness action on the water. It looked like this pair of swans were having a big disagreement.

The female Australasian darter has a creamy coloured chest with yellow and brown beak and feet.

The male Australasian darter, however, is almost entirely black except for a creamy line below the eyes and light coloured beak and feet.

Over on the island in the middle of the pond, the Australasian darter sits on a branch spreading her wings out to dry. Their feathers absorb water so they can dive under water to catch fish to eat. The little black cormorant is resting on the branch beside her as well.

Also on the branches are other little black cormorants. They are very strong swimmers hardly ever seen on land.

Little pied cormorants often dive very quickly underwater to catch fish to eat as well.

The royal spoonbills, also known as the black-billed spoonbills, move their bills from side to side to catch fish, small insects and crustaceans.

The royal spoonbills with the "hair-do" are in breeding plumage.

Just look at the unusual shape of this bird's beak.

The corellas visit the duck ponds as well. They are real characters. I would love to know what this bird is trying to say. What do you think they are saying?

Corellas' diets include seeds.

We saw lots of birds on the grass near the lake as well. They are used to seeing people and don't worry about you being nearby. My grandson loves to get close-up photos of them.

The domesticated geese are not an Australian native but are regular visitors to the duck ponds.

Check out that tongue!

28

There are lots of birds' nests over on the protected island in the middle of the lake. It's a safe distance from the shore keeping people and predators away.

This cattle egret was feeding her hungry chicks.

During breeding season their golden plumage attracts attention.

I have seen cattle egrets feeding on insects that are disturbed as the cattle move.

This baby egret had fallen from its nest. The volunteer carers from ANARRA Wildlife Rescue Gympie check the birds regularly to ensure they are safe and well.

Looking up, I saw a great egret perched high in a tree.

These birds, with a massive wing span of 130 to 170 centimetres, can stand up to one metre tall.

You can see them searching for food on the side of the lake. Their diet includes fish, frogs and lots of other little creatures.

The ibis also goes by the nickname "bin chicken" because they often feed on food scraps from rubbish bins and at the dump.

I think the ibises look quite elegant as they stroll along the edge of the lake.

The magpie goose flies off, leaving the ibises on the side of the lake.

There are always lots of birds beside the lake. This magpie goose is walking alongside a dusky moorhen.

The dusky moorhen's chick stays close to its mother beside the lake.

The moorhen chick jumps up onto the shore. He is very fluffy.

I wonder how they manage to walk on the tree limbs with those massive feet. Spreading their wings would help them balance.

Muscovy ducks are found at the Duck Ponds but did you know they are not native to Australia?

The Pacific black ducks swam on past me. These birds are found in most regions of Australia even in the desert regions! They eat mainly plants but do eat some insects and other animal matter.

The plumed whistling ducks are mainly herbivorous which means they feed mostly on plants. Most of their grazing is done on land. This bird takes a quick dive. Look at the displaced water!

He returns to the surface after the underwater dive, gives a quick shake and the water just runs off his back.

Have you heard that saying - "… like water off a duck's back"?

They are very social ducks and can often be seen in large groups. I reckon they are one of the most stylish birds there is. Fashion designers could use their colour scheme in their creations.

Australian wood ducks (or maned geese) also visit at the Duck Ponds. The bird on the left is the male and the other is the female. When they hatch the chicks have waterproof down.

Hardhead ducks (also known as the white-eyed ducks) are diving ducks that feed mostly on vegetation.   They live in most regions of Australia and are rarely seen on land.

The pelicans occasionally visit the duck ponds searching for food. They eat fish but will also eat ducklings.

Turtles live in the water of the duck ponds but can sometimes be seen sharing a log with birds.

We were very lucky to observe this turtle on the bank because they usually scurry quickly back into the water to safety.

Water dragons are often seen swimming in the water or sunning themselves on land.

It has been lovely WALKING WITH WILDLIFE with you at the Duck Ponds and seeing some water birds. Most of the time I walk on the tracks around my property west of Gympie and I'll be back on my normal track near my home for our next adventure.

Can you name these birds and animals?

Cattle Egret

Dusky Moorhen

Domestic Goose

Little Black Cormorant

Hardhead Duck

Australasian Darter

Ibis

Muscovy Duck

Great Egret

Pied cormorant

Magpie Geese

Water Dragon

Can you name these birds and animals?

- Pacific Black Duck
- Australian Wood Duck
- Turtle
- Cygnet
- Swan
- Spoonbill
- Plumed Whistling Duck
- Pelican
- Corella

www.walkingwithwildlife.com.au

Lots of wildlife in our region are injured and ANARRA (Australian Native Animals Rescue and Rehabilitation Association) volunteers nurse them and provide the care they need. I would like to acknowledge those volunteers who give their time to help our precious wildlife.   www.anarra.org

www.ingramcontent.com/pod-product-compliance
Lightning Source LLC
Chambersburg PA
CBRC102224090526
44583CB00010BA/194